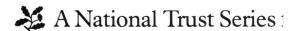 A National Trust Series

For King or Commons

THE INSIDE STORY OF
ROUNDHEADS AND CAVALIERS

Harry T Sutton

BATSFORD – HERITAGE BOOKS

Research: R J Sutton

Design and art direction: Fetherstonhaugh Associates, London

Illustrations: Chapters 1 and 2, Chris Molan; Chapters 2 and 3, Linda Broad, Valerie Headland, Judith Jeffery, Jane Tamblyn

Produced by Heritage Books

Published jointly by B T Batsford Limited and Heritage Books

Distributed by B T Batsford Limited, 4 Fitzhardinge Street, London W1H 0AH

Printed by Robert MacLehose & Co. Ltd, Glasgow

ISBN 0 7134 1727 7

Contents

1 The Battle Nobody Won

'What is wrong with Cary, Nan Fudd?' asked Betty Verney. 'She cries all the time and does not answer when I ask her why.'

'Get on with your sewing, child,' said her nurse. 'What ails your poor sister is no concern of yours.'

'She's in love!' declared Molly Verney. 'That's what ails Cary. And if the silly goose cried less and made herself look prettier Captain Gardiner would marry her. Father wouldn't mind. He would be pleased to get one of us off his hands!'

'Well!' exclaimed Nan Fudd. 'Of all the things to say. I don't know what you modern girls are coming to I'm sure!'

It was a bright winter's day in the year 1642 and the fields round Claydon, the Verneys' country home, were deep in snow. But huge logs burned cheerfully in the great open fireplace and it was warm and snug in the drawing room where the two sisters sat at their work.

Betty, who was nine years old, had some half-finished sewing in her hands and her sister Molly was embroidering a chair cover as they chatted together with their old nurse.

'I hope I get married before I'm an old maid,' sighed Betty. 'Poor Sue and Pen are old maids, aren't they Nan?'

'Your sister, Miss Sue, is only twenty-one and Miss Pen is only twenty,' replied Nan Fudd. 'You cannot call them old maids yet!'

'But Cary is only fifteen and brother Ralph married his Margaret when *she* was only thirteen!'

'Do stop it, Betty!' said her sister. 'Why I'm only fourteen and you are making me feel like an old maid too!'

The Verney family was a big one, six girls and four boys, and whilst they were children, life at Claydon had been all laughter and fun. They lived in a very big house with plenty of servants to clean and cook and wait at table in the big family dining hall. Nan Fudd had been nanny to all of the children since Ralph the eldest son was born so she, of course, was one of the family now. Then there was William Roades the Steward, Mrs Allcock the housekeeper, the cook and her scullery maids; several footmen and goodness knows how many gardeners, grooms and odd job men. The girls all had a maid-servant of their own to brush their hair and help them dress, but they were like family friends too. They came from the village nearby and expected to work for the Great House. They always had; and their mothers and grandmothers before them.

The fact was that Claydon House was deep in the country with very bad roads which became quagmires after heavy rain and the household had to be self-contained, especially in the winter when they were often completely cut off for weeks on end. They had a bakery for their own bread; a dairy for milk and butter; a brewhouse for beer; fishponds where fat carp were raised for the table; a dovecote to supply birds for pigeon pie. They hunted deer for venison in nearby forests; caught partridges and other game with hawks and nets. And, of course, there was a farm which supplied the family and the servants' hall with all the vegetables and fruit they could need.

They not only produced all their own food, there was also a blacksmith's forge, a carpenter's shop, a sawpit and a paint shop. They cut down their own trees for timber and for burning and they had a mill to grind their own corn. It was a fine place in which to grow up. But now, except for little Betty, they *were* all grown up. In 1642, as Betty said, a girl could be an old maid by twenty, so it was no wonder that fifteen-year-old Cary, in love with Captain Gardiner of the dragoons, cried quietly to herself as she waited at snow-bound Claydon. You never could tell – he might still not ask her to be his wife!

Sir Edmund Verney looked out of the window at the crowds of people in the street outside his house in Covent Garden. It seemed that all London had turned against the king. As Knight Marshal to Charles I, Sir Edmund was responsible for the running of the royal palace; he was also a member of Parliament and so was his eldest son, Ralph. They both worked hard for the good of England but now things were going very wrong.

The king had led the country into a war against Scotland and there was fighting in Ireland too. The king needed money for the wars but Parliament had refused to pass the tax laws by which the money could be raised. Then again, England was a Protestant country and had been ever since Henry VIII had quarrelled with the Pope. It was feared that Charles was secretly a Catholic – he had married a Catholic wife – and this made him unpopular with Parliament and with the people as well.

As Sir Edmund left his house to attend Parliament at Westminster, his mind was full of dark thoughts. The country was becoming divided because of this quarrel with the king. Those who opposed him and supported Parliament were becoming known as 'Roundheads' and 'Puritans' whilst those who supported the king were being called 'Cavaliers' and 'Royalists'. To Sir Edmund this seemed a sad state of affairs for he believed that Parliament and the King should be partners in government, not enemies.

Now, as he came to Westminster and saw crowds outside the House of Commons, his heart sank.

'No good will come of this day,' he said to himself. And he

pushed through the crowd to take his place in the House.

Sir Edmund's son, Ralph, was also in the Commons that cold winter day and he watched with his father as King Charles made the last foolish move which was to lead to civil war. Desperate to force the Commons to pass the new tax laws, the king had accused the five leading members who opposed them of high treason. He had demanded their arrest but his demands had been ignored and now he had decided to arrest them himself, by force if necessary. Whilst the House was sitting that afternoon, Sir Edmund and his son saw the doors flung open. The King entered with four hundred swordsmen – the first time that a king had ever set foot in the House of Commons.

'I order the arrest of John Pym, John Hampden, William Strade, Sir Arther Haslerigg and Denzil Holles,' he declared in a loud voice. But the Commons had been given warning of the King's intentions and the five men had already made their escape. The members of the House looked on in amusement as the King's guards searched the chamber.

'I see that the birds have flown!' said the king at last. Then, turning, he stamped angrily out of the House. As he went cries followed him of 'privilege, privilege, privilege!' from the laughing Members. And Sir John Edmund looked sadly at his son who was shouting as loudly as the rest. Parliament did indeed have the right of privilege, given centuries before, that none of its members could be arrested in the House.

'It will mean war!' said Sir Edmund, turning to his son.

'Parliament must stand up for its rights,' replied Ralph.

'Even against your King?' asked Sir Edmund.

'Aye,' said his son. 'For I am a Parliament man.'

'And my duty is to the King,' said Sir Edmund.

For that simple word 'privilege' had split England. It had turned a son into a Roundhead and his father into a Cavalier.

'Pray God a way is found to peace,' said Sir Edmund Verney, as, sick at heart, he made his way to Whitehall and his duty as Knight Marshal to the King.

Cary Verney, although she was only fifteen, was a girl with a mind of her own. She thought of Captain Gardiner, Sir Thomas,

as her 'brave Cavalier' and was determined to become his wife. Her father had agreed to the match and so had his. All that now lay between them was his duty as a soldier which until now had kept him away from her, for the captain had been fighting for the king in his war against the Scots. But now that was over. Winter was gone and spring flowers were in full bloom. Her cavalier was back from the war and they were to be married at last!

All was bright and happy again at Claydon as her sisters and the maids helped to get ready for her wedding day. The only sadness now was that her mother had died only two years before.

'How she would have enjoyed it all!' sighed Cary as the wedding dress was prepared. Her father had sent her some beautiful things which had been her mother's. There were lace collars and cuffs, laced handkerchiefs, lengths of lawn with lace along the edge all beautifully rolled up in paper and many other fineries. There were many lace-makers in the villages nearby for this was the centre of the lace industry at that time.

'You must keep all these beautiful things with great care to pass on to *your* children,' Nan Fudd told her as she packed them ready to send off to her new home. And Cary had blushed with pleasure at the thought of a family of her own, five children perhaps, or even ten, and a brave cavalier to father them all!

Across the fields from Claydon lay another fine country house. This was Hillesden House where lived the Denton family, cousins of the Verneys and their very great friends. They had grown up together and were like one big family, even though a horse ride of three miles separated their two homes. It was the addition of their cousins to all the sisters and servants of Claydon which made such a big crowd to see Cary off when she went to London to be married. All the presents, her belongings and clothes she needed as the wife of a soldier, a gallant cavalier, had been sent in advance by horse waggon. Cary and the servants who went with her travelled on horse-back.

'Goodbye dear Cary!'

'Farewell sister, God go with you!'
'Come back and see us all soon!'

With the loving words of her sisters and cousins ringing in her ears, pretty little fifteen-year-old Cary set off to be married It was the happiest, yet nearly the saddest day in her life and although she laughed as she rode away, she cried a little too. For she was leaving her childhood behind at Claydon. And that was something she could never forget – or ever have over again.

For Ralph Verney, the break between Parliament and the King meant taking sides against his father and against most of his friends. He could not be a Royalist, a Cavalier, when he believed that the King was wrong. Yet his father must take the king's side for he had served him as Knight Marshal for many years. His brothers, Edmund and Tom, were officers in the King's army so they must support the Royalists too.

His brother Edmund had written him a cruel letter which had made him very sad.

'Brother,' he had written. 'What I feared is proved too true, which is your being against the King; give me leave to tell you in my opinion 'tis most unhandsomely done and it grieves my heart to think that my father already and I who so dearly love and esteem you, should be bound in consequence (because of our duty to our King), to be your enemy.'

There was however, some good news. Cary was now married and living happily with her Cavalier at his family home. Ralph had received a letter from the newly married couple when they were on their honeymoon. Travelling on horseback with their servants (only old people who could not ride would travel in coaches; they were slow, unsprung and uncomfortable), they had stopped the night at Welwyn where there was an inn on the Great North Road, twenty miles from London. They had sent him their love and he had written back to wish them good luck.

The news from Claydon, however, was not so good. Some of his sisters had been ill with the smallpox but his father had been there and with old Nan Fudd as well to look after them,

the girls were making a good recovery. Ralph was beginning to hope that life could go on just as before and there would not be a clash with the king after all. But then came a bombshell.

King Charles had raised his Standard at Nottingham, a signal for all his supporters to come to his aid. He had declared war on Parliament and, even worse news for Ralph, Sir Edmund Verney had been made his standard bearer, an honour earned by his long years of service and he was already at Nottingham with the king.

Lords of manors and country squires all over England were taking down helmets and breastplates from where they had hung as decorations for dining halls and were burnishing them for use once more. Pikes, halberds, swords and pistols – even crossbows and longbows, were brought out and made ready. Farm-workers were armed and given rough training by their masters, either to fight for the King – or against him.

Civil war had begun and the young men of England were either Roundheads or they were Cavaliers. Nobody could stand aside. Certainly not Ralph Verney, Member of Parliament and heir to the Knight Marshal – standard bearer to the King.

For the two young princes, 23 October 1642 promised to be the most exciting day of their lives. Charles, Prince of Wales, who was twelve and his younger brother James had been on the march with their father for several weeks and it seemed that a battle was to be fought at last. The Roundheads had about 10,000 men and the King's army about the same. The Earl of Essex was in command of the Roundheads. King Charles himself was to lead the Cavaliers.

'Our brave men will soon chase that rabble off!' declared Prince Charles.

'They'll chase them all the way to London!' agreed his brother. And the King smiled at their words.

'It will be in the hands of God,' he told them. 'But right is on our side!'

King Charles and his two sons were having breakfast with Sir Edmund Verney at an inn called 'Sun Rising' on the crest of a ridge called Edgehill. With them was Doctor William

Harvey who was surgeon to the king and tutor to the princes, Charles and James.

When breakfast was finished, the king said farewell to his sons, leaving them in the care of their tutor with the warning that he must keep them out of danger. Then buckling on his armour, over which he wore a splendid velvet cloak bearing the royal insignia of the Star and Garter, he set off with Sir Edmund and his gentlemen-at-arms, to take command of the battle soon to start.

Sir Edmund Verney knew that he was about to die. When the king first asked him to bear the standard he had been honoured and hopeful for the royalist cause. He had written home to Claydon for his arms. The old breastplate and backplate, the 'pot' helmet, the sword which his grandfather took into battle for Queen Elizabeth, his flintlock pistol. But now, as the Battle of Edgehill approached, the old knight had lost heart.

It was not fear of being on the losing side which put dread into Sir Edmund's heart that bright autumn day. After so many years of peace, neither side was experienced in the arts of war and even though not as well armed as the Roundheads, the Cavaliers were not a whit less brave or gallant. The black thoughts which were with Sir Edmund as he rode beside the king, the royal standard held proudly aloft, were of a different kind.

He hated the Civil War which had turned his son into his enemy. He dreaded the killing and destruction which was about to fall upon England – the country he loved and for which he would soon die. He was the King's man, body and soul – but he could not believe in the King's cause. Sir Edmund was at heart a Parliament man, like Ralph, but after thirty years serving the king he could not forsake him now.

So it was that when Sir Edmund went into battle he was not wearing his armour or his helmet. He held the standard. And he carried the sword with which to defend it to the last. But that was all. He did not choose to defend his own life as well.

Doctor Harvey and the princes watched the battle from the top

of Edgehill. It was a grandstand view for the land fell away steeply from where they stood and they could see the Roundhead army laid out below them like toy soldiers on a carpet of green. There were guns on the ridge nearby which fired from time to time and the princes could see the heavy iron balls volleying towards the enemy, sometimes cutting through them leaving swathes of fallen men behind. More often dropping harmlessly into open ground.

The princes saw their father riding down the lines of Cavaliers and heard him tell them as he rode: 'Your king bids

you be courageous and heaven make you victorious!'

Then the Cavaliers rode down the hill, their horses slipping and sliding on the steep grass slopes. The musketeers and pikemen quickly followed on foot and the guns were hauled down behind them with ropes. The battle began with a cavalry charge. Prince Rupert, the king's nephew, was in command of the horsemen on the army's right flank and as soon as the signal was given – four rounds fired from the guns – he led his force of nearly fifteen hundred mounted men into a gentle trot, then into a canter. They rode straight towards the Roundhead cavalry and dragoons. Then a trumpet sounded the 'charge!' and their horses broke into a full gallop.

Scrambling down the hill to get a closer view, the two princes cheered the gallant charge.

''Tis Rupert!' exclaimed the Prince of Wales. 'He will see them off!' and the boys waved their hats and cheered again.

Prince Rupert had already proved his bravery in a small skirmish with the Roundheads a few days before. Now, at the head of his Cavaliers he was proving his valour once again.

The Roundhead cavalry and dragoons stood firm at first. They fired their pistols at the galloping Cavaliers but they had little effect. Soon they had drawn their swords and were fighting for their lives. Then, overwhelmed by the strength of the attack, they began to retreat. At first they moved back slowly but within minutes the Roundheads were in full flight, racing as hard as their horses could gallop away from the shouting, slashing, cutting Cavaliers.

Prince Rupert's men chased the Roundheads off the field far to the rear and it should have been a famous victory. But soon they came to the village of Kineton, almost three miles from Edgehill. There they found the Roundheads' baggage train – heavy waggons loaded with all the belongings of the enemy's troops and food for them to eat after the battle. They found the Roundhead general's coach and in it valuables and money.

The cavaliers had not been paid for many weeks and they had not eaten for forty-eight hours. Here was loot for the taking and so easily captured that Rupert could not stop his men.

The brave cavalry charge ended in a plundering scramble, whilst in the battle far behind there began a fearsome clash of arms.

For Doctor William Harvey, the day had been long and tiring. He was not interested in war and it so happened that he was particularly interested just then in a little book written by a medical colleague which had to do with the function of the heart. The Doctor was famous for his discovery of the circulation of the blood and, sitting now quite comfortably in a ditch at the base of Edgehill, he was quite unaware of the battle growing in noise and ferocity around. Seeing their tutor busy with his book, the two princes went off together to get a better view. They were just in time for a Roundhead attack on the Cavalier lines.

The method of war at this time was for foot soldiers to meet on the battlefield for hand to hand fighting – 'to push of pike' – and this is what now happened at Edgehill. The foot soldiers clashed and then, galloping through their lines, the Roundhead horsemen rode into battle, slashing and hacking at the Royalist troops who began to retreat and then to run before them. The centre of the king's army began to move back and soon there was a danger to the King himself as he stood in the rear with his gentlemen-at-arms and his standard bearer, the King's personal flag held bravely aloft.

As the battle surged towards them, Sir Edmund stood firm, then he advanced with the standard, leading the retreating men back into the fight. Soon he was surrounded by the enemy. Three Roundheads he cut down with his sword as they tried to capture his precious flag.

'We offer you your life,' shouted one Roundhead officer, 'in exchange for the standard!'

'My life is my own,' Sir Edmund replied, 'but the standard is my King's. I shall not give it up whilst I live!'

Sir Edmund was killed. But even in death he held fast to the royal standard.

'Hack off his hand!' ordered a Roundhead. And the faithful standard bearer's hand was cut off so that the flag could be wrested from his grasp.

So the battle raged on. The two princes were nearly caught up in the fighting and Prince Charles was shouting 'I fear them not!' when Dr Harvey, suddenly realising that his charges had gone, dashed up to them and took them away to a safer place.

The Battle of Edgehill dragged on until dusk. Neither side could force a victory but 4,000 men were left dead on the field. It was the start of bad times for the Roundheads – but of even worse times for the Cavaliers.

The rest of the story is quickly told. Sir Edmund's body was never found but his severed hand with a ring on one of the fingers was recovered and brought to Claydon. It was clear evidence of his bravery and his death, for the ring had been

given to the Knight Marshal by the king. It had a tiny portrait of King Charles in place of a stone. The ring became a treasured possession of the Verneys of Claydon and can be seen now by visitors to Claydon House.

Poor little Cary's cavalier husband was killed in the war and she bore his child two months after his death. Ralph Verney after his father's death could no longer support the Roundhead cause – but nor could he be a Cavalier. He chose exile in France rather than fight a war in which he did not believe and his five sisters with Cary and her baby were left alone at Claydon in the care of the housekeeper and the steward, Roades.

A year after Sir Edmund's death, the house at Hillesden was attacked by Roundheads and burned to the ground. Their cousins went to live with the Verney girls at Claydon and they stayed, women and children sheltering from war whilst battles were fought in the hills and fields all around. It was a bad time for England. Civil war is the worst tragedy that a country can endure.

Oliver Cromwell became dictator – he was known as Protector of the Commonwealth – and King Charles was tried and

executed for being the cause of the war. Britain was without a king for more than ten years but then came the restoration of the monarchy and the Prince of Wales, after waiting all those years in exile, became Charles II. After him, his brother James became king as well, so it was just as well that Dr Harvey found them at Edgehill in time, for two future kings of England were in his care that day!

Ralph Verney, now Sir Ralph and head of the family, came back to Claydon. Cary was married again to a rich landowner in Hampshire who made her happy at last. Her sisters, Sue, Pen Molly, Mary and Betty never did become old maids. They all married and had children of their own to live into the better days ahead. It had been a war that nobody wanted. But it taught both King and Commons that they must govern together in mutual respect.

2 The Inside Story

The Civil War which brought such troubles to the Verneys and their friends, dragged on for five long years. Twenty-six separate battles were fought; more than ten castles were attacked and many of them totally destroyed; dozens of houses were turned into fortresses from which garrisons could make raids into the surrounding countryside. Many of them, like Hillesden House near Claydon, were attacked and destroyed. Towns were besieged; villages looted and their men taken to serve as soldiers for King or Parliament. Many wicked and cruel things were done; and many brave and gallant things as well.

Both sides in the quarrel were really fighting for the same things – law, justice and the right to worship God in their own particular way. The Roundheads thought that Parliament should have the power to enforce these simple things. The Cavaliers believed that the right should belong to the king. The Inside Story shows what it meant to the people who had to fight because neither side could settle the quarrel except by war.

THE COUNTRYSIDE

If you were suddenly transported to Britain at the time of the Roundheads and Cavaliers, you would see a very strange country indeed. In the first place there would be very few people about. The whole population only amounted to about four and a half million; half the number of people who live in Greater London now. Great forests spread over thousands of acres which have since been cleared for farming. The fields were open without fences and, of course, nobody had yet invented barbed wire. Boundaries between farms were marked mainly by ditches or banks and the quickest way to travel from one village to the next was on a horse – straight across country with the steeple of the village church as the landmark to show you the way. Horse racing across the fields from steeple to steeple was a popular country sport which gave the name to our modern 'steeplechase'.

Travel on the roads, however, was not nearly such fun for they were simply deep-rutted tracks, mended here and there by the local parish whose duty it was to keep them in good repair with a few stones and gravel to fill in the worst potholes and ruts. When the King's army was on the move before the battle of Edgehill with a convoy of heavy waggons carrying army supplies, it took them six full days to travel a distance of sixty miles. One or two of our modern 'juggernaut' lorries could probably carry all the baggage from all the waggons in one load and travel the sixty miles in less than one hour (if there were no traffic police about!).

There were castles, many of them left over from Norman

times, dotted about the countryside. They had moats round them and drawbridges which could still be made to work. They were considered old-fashioned even then and no match for the new cannons which could fire heavy iron balls to knock down their walls. But they could still be used as strong-points and it took time to drag heavy guns along the roads to mount a siege.

Villages were tiny then; mostly a few cottages clustered round a church with the Great House which gave the villagers work not far away. Towns, too, were small and many of them still had high walls round them and gates which could be shut and barred at night.

But, most important of all, the old days of the barons who ruled great areas of the country almost independently of the king had not entirely gone. There were still powerful landowners who were able to impose their will in whole counties, villages and towns. Some of these now came out in support of Parlia-

ment and others took the side of the King. This is how England and Wales were divided in May 1643:

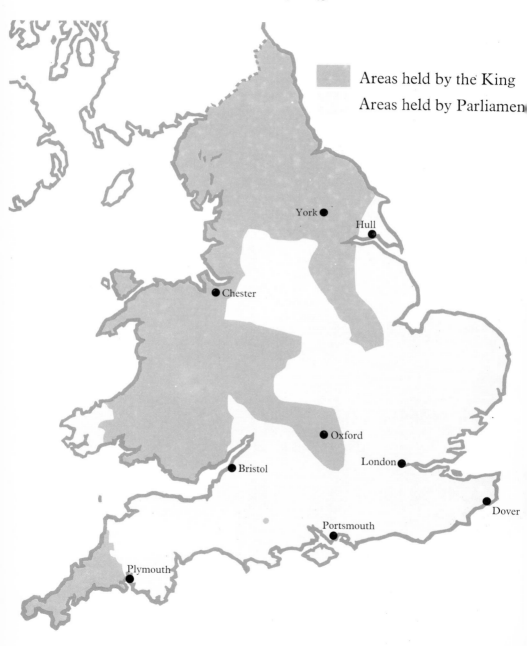

Areas held by the King

Areas held by Parliamen

THE MEN

These days we are used to having a regular army, navy and air force. They are much smaller in peacetime, of course, than in time of war. But they are always there and the men and women in them make the services their career.

At the time of the Civil War, there was no regular army and there had been no major wars in England for over a hundred years. There had been wars in Europe and British mercenaries (paid by foreign countries to fight for them) had fought for Holland, Spain, France and Sweden, so that there were some professional soldiers trained in the arts of war. There were also the 'trained bands' which were units raised by each county for its own defence. These troops, who drilled for a few days each year, were not expected to serve outside their counties; they did not wear uniforms but there were at least weapons for them which they were taught to use in case of war.

When King Charles raised his standard at Nottingham the only troops he had were some horse guards called the 'gentlemen pensioners' and his Yeomen of the Guard. He raised the great army which fought at Edgehill by issuing orders called 'commissions of array' which was an ancient right the King had to require his supporters to recruit men to fight for him. The King now gave these commissions to rich and powerful men in every county and they in turn commissioned some of their followers (often their own sons) as colonels to raise volunteers 'by beat of drum'. This meant going round the towns and villages with a drummer calling on men to join the King's army. (We still speak of 'drumming up' support for something.) The pay offered by the recruiting officers was 30p a week for musketeers, 68p for dragoons and 75p for horsemen. Men from the trained bands were the first to volunteer and then a flood of men came forward to the King's support.

Parliament raised its army in a similar way. The main difference was that whereas the King had no money and relied upon his supporters to pay for the army they raised, Parliament could vote the money they needed and raise it by taxes. They could pay for the recruiting of their men but the pay they offered their recruits was exactly the same as that offered to

recruits for the King.

Charles had raised his standard at Nottingham on August 22 and the Battle of Edgehill was fought only two months later, on October 23. In that short time, both sides had raised armies of 10,000 men. It is not really surprising that the battle ended as it did. For nearly all the troops of both sides, it was their very first experience of war.

THE WEAPONS
Pistols and muskets

Pistols and muskets at this time were loaded through the open end of the barrel. Loose gunpowder was poured in, then the 'shot' and iron ball, then a wad of rag or paper was rammed down on top with a ramrod and the musket was ready to be fired.

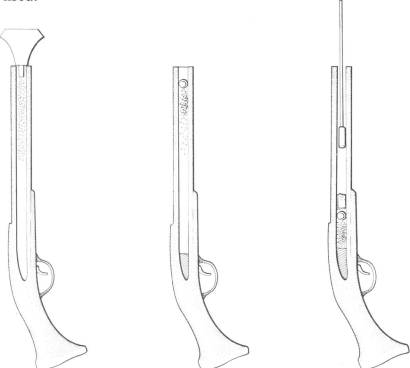

This meant that the gunpowder imprisoned inside the barrel had somehow to be set on fire so that it would explode and shoot the ball out of the barrel. This was done by leaving a tiny hole at the closed end of the barrel above the gunpowder called the 'touch hole' through which a hot flame could be sent to explode the gunpowder.

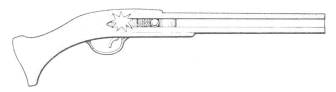

The flame was made by pouring some more gunpowder into a 'pan' on top of the touch hole and then setting it off. The musketeers did this by means of a length of rope soaked in saltpetre to make it smoulder. This was called the 'match' and it was lit at both ends. One lighted end was then fixed to the 'cock' which snapped the match down into the powder in the pan when the trigger was pressed.

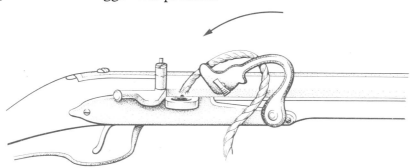

This, of course, fired the gun. This kind of musket was called a 'matchlock'. It was very clumsy to load as you can see and a musketeer using one was lucky if he could fire three rounds in a minute. A well-aimed shot might hit a man sixty yards away.

On horseback, of course, it was difficult enough to load a musket or pistol with powder and shot without having to fix a lighted match in place, so the cavalry carried 'wheel-lock' or 'flintlock' pistols or muskets. The wheel lock was wound up with a key against a powerful spring and when it was released by the trigger, a serrated ring around the wheel turned against a

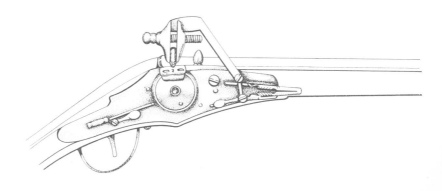

piece of flint sending a stream of sparks into the pan.

The flintlock simply had a piece of flint clamped into the cock which, when released by the trigger, snapped down on to a steel plate causing a spark to flash into the pan full of powder.

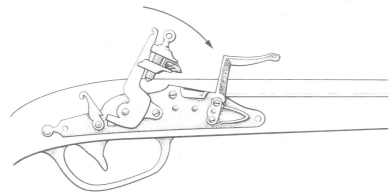

Sometimes it misfired and the powder in the pan burned but did not set off the main charge in the barrel. It is from this that we get the expression 'only a flash in the pan' for something that does not quite come off.

Pikes
At the Battle of Edgehill serious fighting did not really begin

until the foot soldiers met and fought at 'push of pike'. This was considered to be the proper way to fight a battle and for a long time field guns were considered very 'unsporting' because the gunners never saw the men they killed, face to face. Pikes were sixteen feet long and made of ash with a steel head attached to the wooden shaft by metal straps. There were four types of pike:

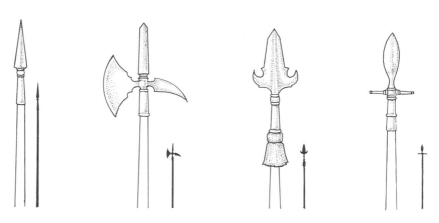

From left to right: the type carried by the ordinary pikemen; the 'halberd', carried by the sergeants; the 'partisan', used by officers; the 'spontoon', which was also carried by officers and was sometimes called a 'half-pike'.

The artillery

The guns used during the Civil War were of all different shapes and sizes. Modern field guns have to be standardised so that they can be mass-produced. As few different sizes as possible are used so that the ammunition can be mass-produced as well.

The guns used by the Cavaliers and Roundheads varied from a 'cannon royal' which fired a sixty-three pound shot, to a 'robinet' which fired a shot weighing only three quarters of a pound. At Edgehill, King Charles had a total of twenty guns of which two were tiny robinets, twelve were fawcons and fawconetts which fired $2\frac{1}{2}$ and $1\frac{1}{2}$ lb shots; four were culverins and demi-culverins firing fifteen pound and nine pound shots; and the only two big guns were two demi-cannons which fired shots weighing twenty-seven pounds. They were loaded in exactly the same way as a musket with a touch hole leading to the main charge.

Each gun was served by a gunner and his mate with one or more labourers to help carry the shot and move the gun to new sites during the battle. They fired 'round shot' or cannon balls but could also be loaded with canisters of musket balls, which were very deadly fired at short range against men in close formation.

The guns were usually sited in the intervals between formations of foot-soldiers. The heavier guns were sometimes placed behind the infantry to fire over their heads. The guns the two princes saw firing at Edgehill were placed halfway up the hill but they were not of much use because, instead of bowling along the ground when they landed, their cannon balls fell almost vertically and buried themselves in the soft ground.

HOW THEY FOUGHT
The cavalry
It was the Royalist cavalry officers who earned the Cavaliers their fame as gallant fighters. They were mostly country gentlemen who joined the King's side and, of course, they had been taught to ride across country as boys, hunting the fox. Now as Royalist officers, they were splendidly dressed for battle. They wore feathers in their helmets, they carried silver-mounted swords and pistols, they wore steel breast-plates over

which they wore a scarf of a colour to show that they were fighting for the King. And, of course, they were mounted on their own hunters which could jump hedges and ditches when charging the enemy as easily as chasing foxes.

They were the officers. The men they led on horseback, the troopers, were not quite as well dressed or as well mounted. But they were just as brave, and, being country men, many of them were tenants on the land which belonged to their officers, and they also learned to ride in the hunting field.

Most of the Roundhead officers were also country-born gentlemen, but their troopers were not. At their first meeting with the Cavaliers, the Roundhead horsemen did badly and Oliver Cromwell, who was himself a cavalry officer, said this to a fellow officer: 'Our troopers are most of them old, decayed servingmen and tapsters and such kind of fellows, whilst *their* troopers are gentlemen's sons, younger sons and persons of quality; do you think that the spirit of such base and mean fellows will be ever able to encounter gentlemen that have honour and courage and resolution in them? You must get men of a spirit that is likely to go on as far as a gentleman will go or else I am sure you will be beaten still.' What he meant, of course, was that the London townsmen who made up most of the Roundhead cavalry, had never enjoyed foxhunting. But being gentlemen's sons and persons of quality did not stop Prince Rupert's troopers from looting the baggage trains at Edgehill.

There were other mounted men in both services called 'dragoons'. These were really infantrymen who used horses to travel more quickly to where they were needed in the battle. Then they dismounted and fought on foot.

Infantry

The foot soldiers on both sides were of two kinds – musketeers and pikemen. Their way of fighting needed two musketeers to one pikeman in each company. This is how they fought. The musketeers could not reload their weapons quickly, so to have time for this, they fought in several lines:

The first rank fired, then whilst they were re-loading, the rear rank moved forward through them and fired in their turn.

When they had fired they re-loaded and the next rear rank came forward and fired, and so on.

By this means the musketeers actually moved forward, rank by rank, towards the enemy. In retreat, the front rank moved to the rear after firing and re-loaded.

In order to train their men to fire their muskets, they did 'musket drill' just as modern soldiers have arms drill for when they are on parade. This was the drill for 'giving fire!':

Because pikes were sixteen feet long and very heavy, only very tall strong men were chosen to be pikemen. They also had a drill:

If the infantry was attacked by cavalry (as they were at Edgehill) they formed a circle with the pikemen inside and the musketeers outside. With the long pikes stretching over their heads, the musketeers crouched down and if they had time to re-load fired off their muskets from a kneeling position. The cavalry would thus find themselves faced with a very prickly hedgehog which could sting!

THE NEW MODEL ARMY

In order to fight well, soldiers need plenty of food, rest between battles, good weapons and a sure supply of ammunition. They also need regular pay so that their families can buy food and clothing and, of course, good generals to lead them to victory.

For the first three years of the Civil War, neither side ever had all of these things at the same time. Prince Rupert was a good cavalry general but his men were badly paid and in order to feed them he had to let them find food for themselves from shopkeepers in towns and farmers in the country – by force if necessary. The Earl of Essex was also a good general and, because Parliament was able to raise the money he needed, his troops were paid regularly. Nevertheless, the men were badly trained and were led by Members of Parliament who knew nothing about fighting or leading men.

Eventually, the Civil War was brought to an end when Parliament decided to correct all these mistakes. First they passed a law which required all Members of Parliament to resign from army commands. Then another which allowed the formation of a standing army of regular soldiers such as we have today. It was to be called the New Model Army. It would have standard rates of pay and the men would be properly trained and led by officers who had learned the arts of war.

By June 1645 the New Model Army numbered 22,000 well-trained men and when the Battle of Naseby was fought on 14 June, King Charles's infantry and all his munitions were captured. These losses made it impossible for King Charles to carry on the war and, although there were a few more battles, the people of Britain did not have long to wait for peace. Charles I surrendered at Newark on 5 May 1646.

Travelling these days through the peaceful countryside it is difficult to imagine that only three hundred years ago armies were marching, guns firing and battles were being fought in places where people now go for quiet country walks!

3 See Where It Happened

A Civil War is a terrible thing to happen to a country. As we have seen it divides the nation and can even set members of the same family against each other. Such a war is not easily forgotten and there are still many reminders left in Britain of the conflict between Roundheads and Cavaliers. At the Banqueting Hall, Whitehall in London for example, you can still see the window where Charles I stepped out on to the scaffold to be executed. In the Tower of London you can examine the different types of armour and weapons that the armies used. You can see the damage that was done to the great castles of the country – Corfe Castle in Dorset and Kenilworth Castle in Warwickshire are only two. You can explore old battlefields like Edgehill in Warwickshire, Marston Moor in Yorkshire, and Naseby in Northamptonshire, which are all marked by monuments.

However, the best way to discover what it was really like to live through the Civil War is to visit the country homes of the old families of England. In them you can see portraits of the men and women who lived at the time. You can learn about what happened to them in the war, and you can see the kind of homes they had. Many of these houses are now owned by the National Trust. The Trust likes to preserve them as living monuments and so many of the old families, whose ancestors fought in the Civil War, still live in the houses. Here is a list of National Trust properties you can visit which have a tale to tell about the days of Roundheads and Cavaliers.

Antony House, Cornwall

During the Civil War, Antony House belonged to the Carew family. When they had to decide which side to support, the family was divided like the Verneys at Claydon. Sir Alexander Carew, the head of the family, supported Parliament and the rest of the family were so angry that they cut his portrait out of its frame. Later Sir Alexander considered changing sides but he was executed before he could do so. His brother, John Carew, was a Roundhead too. He was executed when Charles II returned in 1660. The present house was built much later in 1721, but you can still see Sir Alexander's portrait and the marks where it was cut out.

Beningbrough Hall, North Yorkshire
Sir John Bourchier lived here at the time of the Civil War. He decided to join the Roundheads because he had been imprisoned by the King's favourite, Strafford. He was one of the men who signed Charles I's death warrant. The present house was built in 1716, but it is on the site of the older one that Sir John knew.

Charlecote Park, Warwickshire
In the park surrounding the house there is a meadow beside the River Avon. It was here that Charles I and his army camped the night before the Battle of Edgehill in 1642. Charlecote was probably the last country house Sir Edmund Verney saw before he was killed. In the Great Hall you can see Oliver Cromwell's

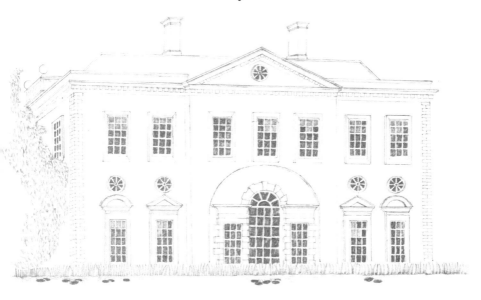

Claydon House, Buckinghamshire

Dunster Castle, Somerset

signature on a summons to the owner of Charlecote, Richard
Lucy, to attend the Parliament of 1653. You can also see
Richard Lucy's passport which he used during the Civil War.
It is signed by General Waller – a Roundhead. Richard's
brother, Spencer Lucy, had been a Cavalier.

Claydon House, Buckinghamshire

The house that Sir Edmund Verney knew no longer exists.
The present one was built much later, in 1754. You can see a
portrait of Sir Edmund and in the library there are three
letters written by Charles I and one by Cromwell.

Coughton Court, Warwickshire,

This was the home of the Throckmorton family who were
Catholics. During the Civil War they supported the King. In
1643 the Roundheads laid siege to the house and captured it.
The next year the Royalists did a lot of damage when they
bombarded the house with artillery.

After the Restoration the family were able to return to
Coughton.

Croft Castle, Herefordshire

Sir William Croft, owner of the castle, was a Royalist. In 1645 he was chased by Roundheads from Stokesay to the grounds of Croft Castle and was killed just before he reached safety. Later, much of the castle was destroyed by the Royalists themselves to prevent it falling into enemy hands.

Dunster Castle, Somerset

Dunster was an important castle in Somerset. Both sides tried to capture it during the Civil War. The Royalists attacked it twice – in 1642 and in 1643. Prince Charles came here when he was fifteen, three years after his adventure at Edgehill. He was trying to gather support for his father. You can see the room in the castle where he slept. At the end of the war the castle was under siege by the Roundheads for 160 days. The Royalists inside finally surrendered after a dramatic fight. After the war the Roundheads knocked down some of the castle walls. You can see the remains of them today.

East Riddlesden Hall, Keighley, West Yorkshire

James Murgatroyd made sure everyone knew who he supported. On the battlements of his house he carved the motto 'Vive Le Roy 1642' – Long live the King! The words are still there.

Gawthorpe Hall, Lancashire

Richard Shuttleworth, who owned Gawthorpe, was in Parliament when Charles I tried to arrest the five members. He became a colonel in the Roundhead army and was a very successful soldier. One night at Gawthorpe he was woken by the news that the Royalists were approaching. He quickly organised his troops and fought the enemy the next day near Read Hall. The Royalists were defeated and Lancashire remained for Parliament.

Great Chalfield Manor, Wiltshire

When soldiers used private houses as garrisons they demanded food from the local parish. Two hundred Roundheads used this house as a garrison from 1644 to 1646. You can see the accounts for their food in the county archives. In 1645 the garrison at the house held out under a short siege by the Royalists.

Lanhydrock House, Cornwall

The house was owned by Lord Robartes during the Civil War. He was one of the leaders of the Roundheads in the House of Lords. He fought at the Battle of Edgehill and the Battle of Newbury. He became a Field-Marshal. In August 1644 the house was captured by the Royalists and Robartes's children held prisoner. Lord Robartes escaped with the Parliamentary army to Plymouth where he defended the city against the King's troops. No harm came to the children and Lord Robartes lived until 1685.

Oxburgh Hall, Norfolk

The Catholic family of Bedingfeld were Cavaliers. Henry Bedingfeld raised a regiment of infantry and a troop of cavalry from his neighbourhood. The Hall was captured by the Roundheads and badly damaged. You can still see the repairs on the east side of the house. There are charred timbers in the attics too, although these are not open to the public. There is a collection of arms and armour from the time of the Civil War in the armoury.

Powis Castle, Powys, Wales

The castle was defended by William Herbert during the Civil War. The Roundheads finally captured it in 1644. The Herbert family still live in the castle.

St Michael's Mount, Cornwall

The Royalists held the island at the start of the Civil War under Sir Francis Basset. They used the harbour to import arms and supplies from France. In 1644 there were fifty men defending the castle. In 1646 the Roundheads under Colonel Hammond attacked the island. After a fierce fight the Royalists surrendered. You can still see the gap in the cliffs where the Roundheads landed. It is called 'Cromwell's passage'. It must have been a very daring operation. There is some Cromwellian armour in the Chevy Chase room inside the castle. It was discovered near the main door of the castle.

The Vyne, Hampshire
The Vyne was used as a garrison by parliamentary troops. Their commander was Sir William Waller and they took part in the siege of Basing nearby. The siege lasted three years and Basing House was destroyed.

Upton House, Warwickshire
This house did not exist at the time of the Civil War but it is next to the 'Sun Rising' where Charles I had breakfast before the Battle of Edgehill. You can see the area of the battlefield near the house. The 'Sun Rising' is now a private house but it can be seen clearly from the road.

Wilderhope Manor, Salop
Major Thomas Smallman, owner of the manor, was a Royalist. He was captured by Roundheads while on his way to Shrewsbury. They imprisoned him in his own house, but he managed to escape on a horse. There was an exciting chase through the countryside. At a place still called Major's Leap, on Wenlock Edge, his horse was killed, but the brave major got to Shrewsbury safely with his despatches.

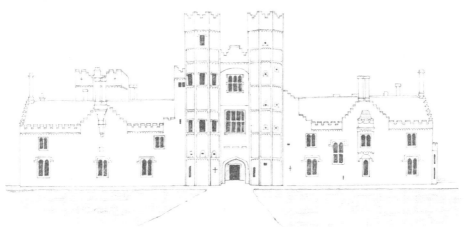

Oxburgh Hall, Norfolk

There are many other houses and castles not owned by the National Trust around the country which were involved in the Civil War. Some are open to visitors and if you visit them try and find out what part they played and how their owners were affected. It was very difficult for families to be neutral in such an important war.

BATTLEFIELDS

The actual sites of Civil War battlefields are marked on Ordnance Survey maps by a cross-swords symbol and the date of the battle. The map on page 48 shows you where the main battles took place. Here is a list of the most important battles and their dates.

Edgehill	1642
Lansdown	1643
Roundway Down	1643
Chalgrove Field	1643
Newbury (first battle)	1643
Cheriton	1644

St Michael's Mount, Cornwall

Marston Moor	1644
Newbury (second battle)	1644
Auldearn	1645
Naseby	1645
Charles I surrenders at Newark	1646

MUSEUMS

Many castles have collections of armour from the Civil War period but the best is in the Tower of London. There is a very interesting section on Roundheads and Cavaliers and the part that London played in the war in the London Museum, in the City of London. Cromwell's old school at Huntingdon, Cambridgeshire, has been made into the Cromwell Museum. There are several exhibits connected with him there. There are other small collections in some of the county museums around the country.

MAP OF PLACES MENTIONED
IN CHAPTER 3

● National Trust properties
⤬ Site of Battle

Beningbrough Hall
⤬ Marston Moor
Hull
East Riddlesden Hall
Gawthorpe Hall

Newark ⤬

Powis Castle
Wilderhope Manor
Naseby ⤬
Oxburgh Hall
Coughton Court
Charlecote Park
Croft Castle
⤬ Upton House
Edgehill
Claydon House
⤬ Chalgrove Field
Great Chalfield Manor
Bristol
Lansdown
⤬ Newbury
London
Roundway Down
The Vyne
Dover
Dunster Castle
⤬ Cheriton
Portsmouth
Lanhydrock House
Plymouth
Antony House
St Michael's Mount